pasta sauces

p

This is a Parragon Book
This edition published in 2005

Parragon
Queen Street House
4 Queen Street
Bath BA1 1HE, UK

ISBN: 1-40543-716-2 (hardback)
ISBN: 1-40543-720-0 (paperback)

Printed in China

Produced by the Bridgewater Book Company Ltd.
Project Designer: Michael Whitehead
Project Editor: Anna Samuels

Notes for the Reader
This book uses metric and imperial measurements. Follow the
same units of measurement throughout; do not mix metric and
imperial. All spoon measurements are level: teaspoons are
assumed to be 5 ml, and tablespoons are assumed to be 15 ml.
Unless otherwise stated, milk is assumed to be full fat, eggs and
individual vegetables such as potatoes are medium, and pepper
is freshly ground black pepper.

Recipes using raw or very lightly cooked eggs should be avoided
by infants, the elderly, pregnant women, convalescents, and
anyone suffering from an illness.

contents

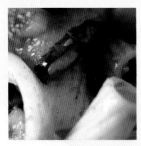

introduction   4

PART ONE
meat & poultry sauces   8

PART TWO
seafood & fish sauces   26

PART THREE
creamy & cheesy sauces   54

PART FOUR
vegetable sauces   74

index   96

introduction

PASTA is one of the easiest dishes to prepare and, combined with a meat, seafood, cheese or vegetable sauce, it makes a delicious meal which can be eaten as a light lunch or as a substantial evening dish. The recipes are also ideal for serving on special occasions at the table or as part of a buffet meal.

Pasta is very popular and versatile. It is cheap and easy to make and can be combined with a wide variety of delicious sauces. Meat and poultry sauces, vegetable sauces or fish and seafood sauces are all excellent pasta accompaniments.

Pasta has existed since the Roman Empire. There are over 200 different pasta types, with new shapes being invented all the time. It is crucial that you combine the right shape of pasta with its sauce. For example, the basic Italian tomato sauce is an excellent sauce for spaghetti, as it is successfully absorbed into the long thin pasta.

Tagliatelle, on the other hand, are ideal for creamy sauces such as the Garlic, Mushroom and Cheese sauce. Pasta shapes are best suited for chunky sauces such as the Tomato, Mushroom and Bacon sauce.

Pasta is made from durum wheat flour and is therefore a good source of protein and carbohydrate and an ideal energy source for those with busy lifestyles. Dried pasta is an ideal storecupboard staple that can be cooked quickly to accompany a sauce. Fresh pasta, though it cooks more quickly, cannot be stored.

To cook pasta the correct way it is best to use a large pan which gives the pasta enough space. Allow 1 litre/3/4 pint of water for every 115 g/4oz pasta. Bring the water to a boil quickly and then add the salt and pasta together, stirring once. The amount of cooking time will depend on the quantity and type of pasta. The pasta will be ready when it is al dente, firm but still slightly chewy. It is easy to overcook pasta so you need to watch out for this. Cook the sauce before you cook the pasta

because if you cook the pasta first there is the risk it will be cold by the time you have finished preparing the sauce! In addition to getting cold, pasta that stands for a while tends to become quite sticky.

In this book the recipes are divided up into recipes for meat sauce, seafood and fish sauces, creamy and cheesy sauces and finally vegetable sauces. All are recipes that you will come back to again and again as they are fun, simple and tasty. They are also easy to prepare and presented with clarity, from the initial preparation stages right through to the final serving of each dish. Each recipe is also accompanied by a photo which clearly shows just how colourful pasta sauces can be.

basic tomato sauce

A sauce that is excellent for any type of pasta and a useful recipe for other dishes.

SERVES 4

2 tbsp olive oil

1 large onion, finely chopped

2 garlic cloves, crushed

280 g/10 oz canned chopped tomatoes

2 tbsp chopped fresh parsley

1 tsp dried oregano

2 bay leaves

2 tbsp tomato purée

salt and pepper

Heat the oil in a large frying pan and fry the onion for 2–3 minutes, or until translucent. Add the garlic and fry for 1 minute. Stir in the chopped tomatoes, parsley, oregano, bay leaves and tomato purée and season to taste with salt and pepper. Bring the sauce to the boil, then simmer for 15–20 minutes.

meat & poultry sauces

MEAT and poultry sauces go particularly well with pasta and are very popular. The seven recipes in this chapter draw on a range of meats and poultry: beef, veal, chicken, lamb, bacon and pork. The recipes are wonderfully varied, from the classic well-known Bolognese sauce to the more unusual Pumpkin Sauce with Parma Ham.

bolognese sauce

You can use this classic meat sauce both to accompany spaghetti,
and for baked pasta dishes such as lasagne and cannelloni. *SERVES 4*

450 g/1 lb dried spaghetti

1 tbsp olive oil

sauce

2 tbsp olive oil

2 garlic cloves, crushed

1 large onion, finely chopped

1 carrot, diced

225 g/8 oz lean minced beef,
veal or chicken

85 g/3 oz chicken livers, finely chopped

100 g/3¹/₂ oz lean Parma ham, diced

150 ml/5 fl oz Marsala

280 g/10 oz canned chopped plum tomatoes

1 tbsp chopped fresh basil leaves

2 tbsp tomato purée

salt and pepper

To make the sauce, heat the olive oil in a large saucepan. Add the garlic, onion and carrot and cook for 6 minutes.

Add the minced meat, chicken livers and Parma ham. Cook over a medium heat for 12 minutes, or until well browned.

Stir in the Marsala, tomatoes, basil and tomato purée and cook, stirring, for 4 minutes. Season to taste. Cover the pan and simmer for 30 minutes. Remove the lid, stir and simmer for a further 15 minutes.

Meanwhile, to cook the pasta, bring a large saucepan of lightly salted water to the boil. Add the spaghetti and oil and cook for 12 minutes, or until tender but still firm to the bite. Drain and transfer to a serving dish. Pour over the sauce and serve.

variation

Chicken livers are an essential ingredient in a classic Bolognese sauce, to which they add richness. However, if you prefer not to use them, you can substitute the same quantity of minced beef, veal or chicken.

tarragon meatball sauce

This well-loved Italian sauce is famous across the world. Make the most of it by using high-quality steak for the meatballs. *SERVES 4*

Place the brown breadcrumbs in a bowl, add the milk and set aside to soak for 30 minutes.

To make the sauce, melt half of the butter in a saucepan. Add the flour and cook, stirring constantly, for 2 minutes. Gradually add the stock and cook, stirring constantly, for a further 5 minutes. Add the tomatoes, tomato purée, sugar and tarragon, reserving a little to garnish. Season well and simmer for 25 minutes.

Meanwhile, mix the onion, minced steak and paprika into the breadcrumbs, and season to taste. Shape the mixture into 16 meatballs.

Heat the oil and remaining butter in a frying pan and cook the meatballs, turning, until brown all over. Place in a deep casserole, pour over the tomato sauce, cover and bake in a preheated oven, 180°C/350°F/Gas Mark 4, for 25 minutes.

To cook the pasta, bring a large saucepan of lightly salted water to the boil. Add the fresh spaghetti, bring back to the boil and cook for about 2–3 minutes, or until tender but still firm to the bite.

Meanwhile, remove the meatballs from the oven and cool for 3 minutes. Serve the meatballs and their sauce with the spaghetti, garnished with the reserved tarragon.

450 g/1 lb fresh spaghetti

meatballs

150 g/5¹/₂ oz brown breadcrumbs

150 ml/5 fl oz milk

1 large onion, chopped

450 g/1 lb minced steak

1 tsp paprika

sauce

2 tbsp butter

3 tbsp wholemeal flour

200 ml/7 fl oz beef stock

400 g/14 oz canned chopped tomatoes

2 tbsp tomato purée

1 tsp sugar

1 tbsp chopped fresh tarragon

salt and pepper

4 tbsp olive oil

sun-dried tomato sauce

There is an appetizing contrast of textures and flavours in this satisfying sauce,
making it a particularly good accompaniment for pasta. *SERVES 4*

500 g/1 lb 2 oz minced lean beef

55 g/2 oz soft white breadcrumbs

1 garlic clove, crushed

2 tbsp chopped fresh parsley

1 tsp dried oregano

pinch of freshly grated nutmeg

$1/4$ tsp ground coriander

55 g/2 oz Parmesan cheese, freshly grated

2–3 tbsp milk

plain flour, for dusting

3 tbsp olive oil

400 g/14 oz dried tagliatelle

2 tbsp butter, diced

sauce

3 tbsp olive oil

2 large onions, sliced

2 celery sticks, thinly sliced

2 garlic cloves, chopped

400 g/14 oz canned chopped tomatoes

125 g/4$1/2$ oz sun-dried tomatoes in oil,
drained and chopped

2 tbsp tomato purée

1 tbsp dark muscovado sugar

about 150 ml/5 fl oz white wine or water

salt and pepper

To make the sauce, heat the oil in a frying pan. Add the onions and celery and cook until translucent. Add the garlic and cook for 1 minute. Stir in all the tomatoes, tomato purée, sugar and wine and season to taste with salt and pepper. Bring to the boil and simmer for 10 minutes.

Meanwhile, break up the meat in a bowl with a wooden spoon until it becomes a sticky paste. Stir in the breadcrumbs, garlic, herbs and spices. Stir in the cheese and enough milk to make a firm paste. Flour your hands, take large spoonfuls of the mixture and shape it into 12 balls. Heat the oil in a frying pan and cook the meatballs for 5–6 minutes, or until browned.

Pour the tomato sauce over the meatballs. Lower the heat, cover the pan and simmer for 30 minutes, turning once or twice. Add a little extra wine if the sauce is beginning to become dry.

To cook the pasta, bring a large saucepan of lightly salted water to the boil. Add the pasta, bring back to the boil and cook for 8–10 minutes, or until tender but still firm to the bite. Drain, turn into a warmed serving dish, dot with the butter and toss with 2 forks. Spoon the meatballs and sauce over the pasta and serve immediately.

bucatini with lamb & yellow pepper sauce

This regional speciality is traditionally served with square-shaped macaroni, but this is not widely available (although you may find it in an Italian delicatessen). This recipe uses bucatini instead. *SERVES 4*

4 tbsp olive oil

280 g/10 oz boneless lamb, cubed

1 garlic clove, finely chopped

1 bay leaf

225 ml/8 fl oz dry white wine

salt and pepper

2 large yellow peppers, deseeded and diced

4 tomatoes, peeled and chopped

250 g/9 oz dried bucatini

Heat half the olive oil in a large, heavy-based frying pan. Add the cubes of lamb and cook over a medium heat, stirring frequently, until browned on all sides. Add the garlic and cook for a further 1 minute. Add the bay leaf, pour in the wine and season to taste with salt and pepper. Bring to the boil and cook for 5 minutes, or until reduced.

Stir in the remaining oil, peppers and tomatoes. Reduce the heat, cover and simmer, stirring occasionally, for 45 minutes.

Meanwhile, bring a large, heavy-based saucepan of lightly salted water to the boil. Add the pasta, return to the boil and cook for 8–10 minutes, or until tender but still firm to the bite. Drain and transfer to a warmed serving dish. Remove and discard the bay leaf from the lamb sauce and spoon the sauce onto the pasta. Toss well and serve immediately.

creamy chicken sauce

This creamy chicken sauce served with spinach ribbon noodles
makes a very appetizing and satisfying dish. *SERVES 4*

Make the tomato sauce, set aside and keep warm. To make the chicken sauce, melt the butter in a large, heavy frying pan over a medium heat. Add the chicken pieces and almonds and cook, stirring frequently, for about 5–6 minutes, or until the chicken is cooked through.

Meanwhile, pour the cream into a small saucepan, set over a low heat and bring to the boil. Continue to boil for 10 minutes, or until reduced by almost half. Pour the cream over the chicken and almonds, stir well and season with salt and pepper to taste. Remove the pan from the heat, set aside and keep warm.

To cook the pasta, bring a large saucepan of lightly salted water to the boil. Add the pasta, bring back to the boil and cook until tender but still firm to the bite. Fresh tagliatelle will take about 2–3 minutes to cook and dried pasta will take about 8–10 minutes, timed from when the water returns to the boil. Drain the pasta, return to the pan, cover and keep warm until ready to serve.

When ready to serve, turn the pasta into a warmed serving dish and spoon the tomato sauce over it. Spoon the chicken and cream sauce into the centre, sprinkle with the basil leaves and serve.

1 quantity Basic Tomato Sauce (see page 7)
225 g/8 oz fresh or dried green tagliatelle
fresh basil leaves, to garnish

sauce
4 tbsp unsalted butter
400 g/14 oz skinless, boneless chicken breast
    portions, thinly sliced
85 g/3 oz blanched almonds
300 ml/10 fl oz double cream
salt and pepper

carbonara sauce

Ensure that all of the cooked ingredients are as hot as possible before
adding the eggs, so that they cook on contact. *SERVES 4*

425 g/15 oz dried spaghetti
sprigs of fresh sage, to garnish
freshly grated Parmesan cheese,
to serve (optional)

sauce
1 tbsp olive oil
1 large onion, thinly sliced
2 garlic cloves, chopped
175 g/6 oz rindless bacon, cut into thin strips
2 tbsp butter
175 g/6 oz mushrooms, sliced
300 ml/10 fl oz double cream
3 eggs, beaten
100 g/3¹/₂ oz Parmesan cheese, freshly grated
salt and pepper

Warm a large serving dish or bowl. To cook the pasta, bring a large saucepan of lightly salted water to the boil. Add the spaghetti, bring back to the boil and cook for 8–10 minutes, or until tender but still firm to the bite. Drain well, return to the pan and keep warm.

Meanwhile, to make the sauce, heat the olive oil in a frying pan over a medium heat. Add the onion and cook, stirring occasionally, for 2–3 minutes, or until translucent. Add the garlic and bacon and cook until the bacon is crisp. Transfer to the warm dish or bowl.

Melt the butter in the frying pan. Add the mushrooms and cook over a medium heat, stirring occasionally, for 3–4 minutes, or until tender. Return the bacon mixture to the pan. Cover and keep warm.

Combine the cream, eggs and cheese in a large bowl and season to taste.

Working very quickly, tip the spaghetti into the bacon mixture and pour over the eggs. Toss the spaghetti quickly into the egg and cream mixture, using 2 forks, and serve immediately, garnished with sage. If you wish, serve with extra grated Parmesan cheese.

cook's tip

The key to success with this recipe is not to overcook the egg. It is important to keep all the ingredients hot enough to just cook the egg and to work rapidly to avoid scrambling it.

pumpkin sauce
with parma ham

This unusual pasta sauce comes from the Emilia Romagna region
of Italy. Why not serve it with Lambrusco, the local wine? *SERVES 4*

To make the sauce, cut the pumpkin in half and scoop out the seeds with a spoon. Cut the pumpkin into 1-cm/¹/₂-inch dice.

Heat the olive oil in a large saucepan. Add the onion and garlic and cook over a low heat for 3 minutes, or until soft. Add half the chopped parsley and cook for 1 minute.

Add the pumpkin pieces and cook for 2–3 minutes. Season to taste with nutmeg, and salt and pepper. Add half the stock to the pan, bring to the boil, cover and simmer for about 10 minutes, or until the pumpkin is tender. Add more stock whenever the pumpkin is becoming dry and looks as if it might be about to burn.

Add the Parma ham to the pan and cook, stirring, for a further 2 minutes.

Meanwhile, to cook the pasta, bring a large saucepan of lightly salted water to the boil. Add the tagliatelle and olive oil and cook for 12 minutes, or until tender but still firm to the bite. Drain the pasta and transfer to a warm serving dish. Stir the cream into the pumpkin and

250 g/9 oz dried green or white tagliatelle

1 tbsp olive oil

freshly grated Parmesan cheese, to serve

sauce

500 g/1 lb 2 oz pumpkin or butternut squash, peeled

2 tbsp olive oil

1 onion, finely chopped

2 garlic cloves, crushed

4–6 tbsp chopped fresh parsley

pinch of freshly grated nutmeg

salt and pepper

about 300 ml/10 fl oz chicken stock or vegetable stock

115 g/4 oz Parma ham, cut into small pieces

150 ml/5 fl oz double cream

ham sauce and heat through well. Spoon the mixture over the tagliatelle, sprinkle over the remaining parsley to garnish and serve while still hot. Serve the grated Parmesan separately.

cook's tip
Soured cream contains 18–20% fat, so if you are following a low-fat diet you can leave it out of this recipe or substitute a low-fat alternative.

tomato, mushroom & bacon sauce

In this dish, fresh tomatoes make a delicious Italian-style
sauce, which goes particularly well with pasta. *SERVES 2*

1 tbsp olive oil

1 small onion, finely chopped

1–2 garlic cloves, crushed

350 g/12 oz tomatoes, peeled and chopped

2 tsp tomato purée

2 tbsp water

salt and pepper

300–350 g/10¹/₂ –12 oz dried pasta shapes

90 g/3¹/₄ oz lean bacon, de-rinded and diced

40 g/1¹/₂ oz mushrooms, sliced

1 tbsp chopped fresh parsley or 1 tsp chopped fresh coriander

2 tbsp soured cream or natural fromage frais (optional)

Heat the olive oil in a saucepan and fry the onion
and garlic gently over a low heat until soft.

Add the tomatoes, tomato purée and water
to the mixture in the pan, season with salt and
pepper to taste and bring to the boil. Cover and
simmer gently for 10 minutes.

Meanwhile, cook the pasta in a large
saucepan of boiling salted water for 8–10 minutes,
or until just tender. Drain thoroughly and then
transfer to warm serving dishes.

Heat the bacon gently in a frying pan until
the fat runs, add the mushrooms, and continue
cooking for 3–4 minutes. Drain off any excess fat.

Add the bacon and mushrooms to the tomato
mixture, together with the parsley and the soured
cream, if using. Reheat and serve with the pasta.

seafood &
fish sauces

SEAFOOD and fish make excellent ingredients in pasta sauces. The six recipes here draw on a wide range of seafood (prawns, squid, mussels, crab and clams) and offer an array of different flavours. The seven fish sauces include two tasty smoked salmon recipes, a sardine-based sauce and three delicious anchovy-based sauces.

seafood sauce

Fresh clams are available from most good fishmongers. If you prefer, use canned clams, which are less messy to eat but not so pretty to serve. *SERVES 4*

675 g/1 lb 8 oz fresh pasta, or 350 g/12 oz dried pasta

sauce

675 g/1 lb 8 oz fresh clams, or 280 g/10 oz canned clams, drained

2 tbsp olive oil

2 garlic cloves, finely chopped

400 g/14 oz mixed prepared seafood, such as prawns, squid and mussels, defrosted if frozen

150 ml/5 fl oz white wine

150 ml/5 fl oz fish stock

2 tbsp chopped fresh tarragon

salt and pepper

First make the sauce. If you are using fresh clams, you need to scrub them clean and discard any that are already open.

Heat the oil in a large frying pan. Add the garlic and clams and cook for 2 minutes, shaking the pan to ensure that all of the clams are coated in the oil. Add the remaining seafood to the pan and cook for a further 2 minutes.

Pour the wine and stock over the mixed seafood and garlic and bring to the boil. Cover the pan, then lower the heat and simmer for 8–10 minutes, or until the shells open. Discard any clams or mussels that do not open.

To cook the pasta, place in a saucepan of boiling water and cook according to the instructions on the packet, or until tender but still firm to the bite. Drain.

Stir the tarragon into the sauce and season to taste. Transfer the pasta to a serving plate and pour over the sauce.

variation

Red Seafood Sauce can be made by adding
125 ml/4 fl oz tomato purée to the sauce
along with the stock. Follow the same
cooking method.

prawn & vegetable sauce

Shelled prawns from the freezer can become the star ingredient in
this colourful and tasty sauce. *SERVES 4*

To cook the pasta, bring a saucepan of lightly salted water to the boil. Add the spaghetti and half of the olive oil and cook until tender but still firm to the bite. Drain the spaghetti, then return to the pan and toss with the remaining olive oil. Cover and keep warm.

To make the sauce, bring the chicken stock and lemon juice to the boil. Add the cauliflower and carrots and cook for 3–4 minutes. Lift out of the pan and set aside. Add the mangetout to the pan and cook for 1–2 minutes. Remove and set aside with the other vegetables.

Melt half the butter in a frying pan over a medium heat. Add the onion and courgettes and cook for about 3 minutes. Add the garlic and peeled prawns and cook for an additional 2–3 minutes, or until thoroughly heated through.

Add the reserved vegetables and heat through, stirring. Season to taste and stir in the remaining butter.

Transfer the spaghetti to a warm serving dish. Pour over the sauce and add the chopped parsley. Toss well with 2 forks until coated. Sprinkle over the Parmesan cheese and paprika, then garnish with the whole prawns and serve immediately.

225 g/8 oz dried spaghetti, broken into 15-cm/6-inch pieces

2 tbsp olive oil

2 tbsp chopped fresh parsley

25 g/1 oz Parmesan cheese, freshly grated

1/2 tsp paprika

4 whole cooked prawns, to garnish

sauce

300 ml/10 fl oz chicken stock

1 tsp lemon juice

1 small cauliflower, cut into florets

2 carrots, thinly sliced

115 g/4 oz mangetout

4 tbsp butter

1 onion, sliced

225 g/8 oz courgettes, sliced

1 garlic clove, chopped

350 g/12 oz cooked, peeled prawns

salt and pepper

spicy crab sauce

This sauce is probably one of the simplest in the book, yet the result
is as impressive as a sauce that takes a long time to prepare.   *SERVES 4*

350 g/12 oz dried spaghettini

salt and pepper

lemon wedges, to garnish

sauce

1 dressed crab, about 450 g/1 lb

(including the shell)

6 tbsp extra-virgin olive oil

1 fresh red chilli, deseeded and

finely chopped

2 garlic cloves, finely chopped

3 tbsp chopped fresh parsley

2 tbsp lemon juice

1 tsp finely grated lemon zest

Scoop the meat from the crab shell into a bowl. Mix the white and brown meat lightly together and set aside.

To cook the pasta, bring a large saucepan of lightly salted water to the boil. Add the pasta, bring back to the boil and cook for 8–10 minutes, or until tender but still firm to the bite. Drain well and return to the pan.

To make the sauce, heat 2 tablespoons of the olive oil in a frying pan. Add the chilli and garlic. Cook for 30 seconds, then add the crab meat, parsley, lemon juice and lemon zest. Stir-fry over a low heat for a further 1 minute, or until the crab meat is just heated through.

Add the crab sauce to the pasta with the remaining olive oil and season to taste with salt and pepper. Toss together thoroughly, transfer to a warmed serving dish and serve immediately, garnished with lemon wedges.

cook's tip

If you prefer to buy your own fresh crab,

you will need a large crab weighing

about 1 kg/2 lb 4 oz.

saffron mussel sauce

Saffron is the most expensive spice in the world, but you only ever need
a small quantity. This sauce is delicious with tagliatelle or other ribbon pasta. *SERVES 4*

To make the sauce, scrub and debeard the mussels under cold running water. Discard any that do not close when sharply tapped. Put the mussels in a saucepan with the wine and onion. Cover and cook over a high heat, shaking the pan, for 5–8 minutes, or until the shells open.

Drain and reserve the cooking liquid. Discard any mussels that are still closed. Reserve a few mussels in their shells for the garnish and remove the remainder from their shells.

Strain the cooking liquid into a saucepan. Bring to the boil and reduce by about half. Remove from the heat.

Melt the butter in a saucepan. Add the garlic and fry, stirring frequently, for 2 minutes or until golden brown. Stir in the cornflour and cook, stirring, for 1 minute. Gradually stir in the cooking liquid and the cream. Crush the saffron threads and add to the pan. Season with salt and pepper to taste and simmer over a low heat for 2–3 minutes, or until thickened.

Stir in the egg yolk, lemon juice and shelled mussels. Do not let the mixture boil.

To cook the pasta, bring a saucepan of lightly salted water to the boil. Add the pasta and oil and cook according to the instructions on the packet, until tender but still firm to the bite. Drain and transfer to a serving dish. Add the mussel sauce and toss together. Garnish with the chopped parsley and reserved mussels and serve.

450 g/1 lb dried tagliatelle

1 tbsp olive oil

3 tbsp chopped fresh parsley, to garnish

sauce

1 kg/2 lb 4 oz mussels

150 ml/5 fl oz white wine

1 medium onion, finely chopped

2 tbsp butter

2 garlic cloves, crushed

2 tsp cornflour

300 ml/10 fl oz double cream

pinch of saffron threads or saffron powder

salt and pepper

1 egg yolk

juice of ¹/₂ lemon

clam sauce

This is another cook-in-a-hurry recipe that transforms storecupboard ingredients into a dish with style. *SERVES 4*

400 g/14 oz vermicelli, spaghetti or other long pasta

2 tbsp butter

1 tbsp olive oil

2 onions, chopped

2 garlic cloves, chopped

400 g/14 oz clams in brine

125 ml/4 fl oz white wine

4 tbsp chopped parsley

1/2 tsp dried oregano

pinch of grated nutmeg

salt and pepper

sprigs of fresh basil, to garnish

2 tbsp shaved Parmesan, to serve

Bring a large saucepan of lightly salted water to the boil. Add the pasta, bring back to the boil and cook for 8–10 minutes, or until tender but firm to the bite. Drain well, return to the pan and add the butter. Cover and shake. Set the pan aside and keep warm.

Heat the olive oil in a saucepan. Add the onions and cook over a low heat, stirring occasionally, for 5 minutes, or until softened. Stir in the garlic and cook for another minute.

Strain the liquid from the clams and pour half of it into the pan. Discard the remaining liquid and reserve the clams.

Add the wine to the pan. Bring to simmering point, stirring constantly, and simmer for 3 minutes.

Add the clams and herbs to the pan and season to taste with nutmeg and pepper. Lower the heat and cook until the sauce is heated through.

Transfer the pasta to a warmed serving platter and pour the clam sauce over it.

Garnish with sprigs of basil and sprinkle over the Parmesan. Serve hot.

rigatoni with squid sauce

This delicious combination of pasta and squid is excellent for a light summer supper.
If time is limited, use fresh pasta, as it takes less time to cook than dried.
Farfalle and penne would also work well. *SERVES 4*

1 red pepper

1 yellow pepper

1 tbsp sunflower or corn oil

350 g/12 oz prepared squid rings

1 onion, chopped

1 garlic clove, finely chopped

400 g/14 oz canned chopped tomatoes

1/2–1 tsp chilli powder

250 g/9 oz dried rigatoni

2 tbsp chopped fresh basil

salt and pepper

Preheat the grill to medium. Place the peppers on a baking sheet and roast under the grill, turning frequently, for 15 minutes, or until charred and beginning to blacken. Remove with tongs, place in a polythene bag and seal the top. When the peppers are cool enough to handle, rub off the skins, deseed and chop the flesh.

Heat the oil in a heavy-based frying pan. Add the squid rings and stir-fry for 1–2 minutes, or until opaque. Remove the squid and set aside. Add the onion and garlic and cook for 5 minutes, or until soft. Add the tomatoes and peppers and chilli powder to taste, reduce the heat and simmer for 20–25 minutes, or until thickened.

Meanwhile, cook the pasta in a saucepan of lightly salted water for 8–10 minutes, or until tender but still firm to the bite. Just before serving, stir the squid rings and basil into the sauce and season to taste with salt and pepper. Heat through for 2–3 minutes. Drain the pasta, transfer to a serving dish and toss with the sauce. Serve.

variation

Use fresh tomatoes instead of canned
when they are in season. Peel, deseed
and chop 750 g/1 lb 10 oz tomatoes.

cook's tip

Serve this rich and luxurious
dish with salad leaves tossed
in a lemon-flavoured dressing.

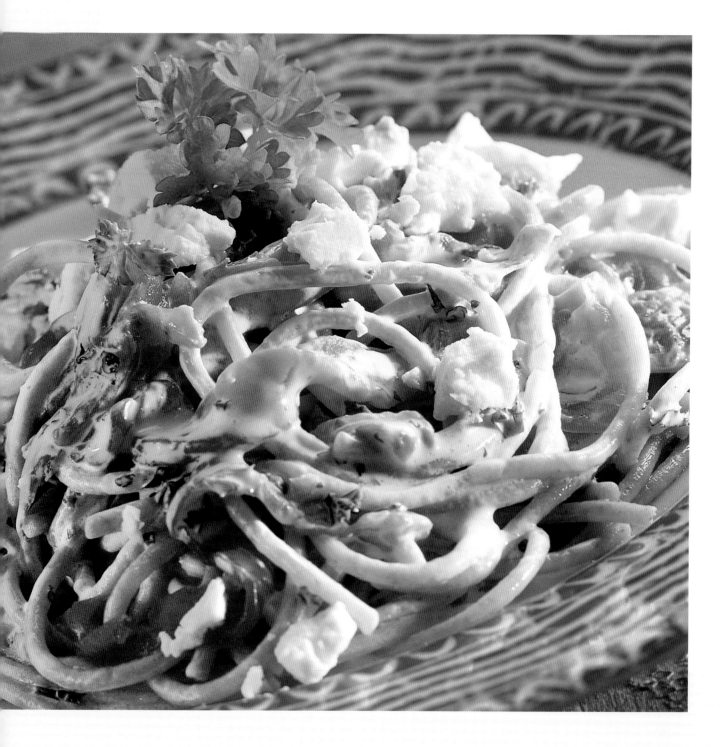

smoked salmon cream sauce

This luxurious sauce is made in moments, and can be used to astonish and delight any unexpected guests. *SERVES 4*

450 g/1 lb dried white or
buckwheat spaghetti

2 tbsp olive oil

to garnish

90 g/3^1/$_4$ oz feta cheese,
well drained and crumbled

sprigs of fresh coriander or parsley

sauce

300 ml/10 fl oz double cream

150 ml/5 fl oz whisky or brandy

125 g/4^1/$_2$ oz smoked salmon

pinch of cayenne pepper

black pepper

2 tbsp chopped fresh coriander or parsley

To cook the pasta, bring a large saucepan of lightly salted water to the boil. Add the spaghetti and half of the olive oil and cook until tender but still firm to the bite. Drain the spaghetti, return to the pan and sprinkle over the remaining olive oil. Cover, shake the pan, set aside and keep warm.

To make the sauce, pour the cream into a small saucepan and bring to simmering point, but do not let it boil. Pour the whisky into another small saucepan and bring to simmering point, but do not let it boil. Remove both pans from the heat and mix the cream with the whisky.

Cut the smoked salmon into thin strips and add to the cream sauce. Season to taste with cayenne and black pepper. Just before serving,

stir in the chopped fresh coriander. Transfer the spaghetti to a warm serving dish, pour over the sauce and toss thoroughly with 2 large forks. To garnish, scatter over the crumbled feta cheese and sprigs of fresh coriander, then serve immediately.

variation

Substitute the same amount of rocket for the watercress, if you like, and garnish with a few sprigs of fresh flat-leaved parsley.

smoked salmon & watercress sauce

This simple dish takes just moments to make, looks lovely, tastes fabulous and contains absolutely no saturated fat – what more could you possibly want? *SERVES 4*

Bring a large saucepan of lightly salted water to the boil over a medium heat. Add the pasta, return to the boil and cook for 8–10 minutes, or until tender but still firm to the bite.

Meanwhile, heat the olive oil in a large non-stick frying pan. Add the garlic and cook over a low heat, stirring constantly, for 30 seconds. Add the salmon and watercress, season to taste with pepper and cook for a further 30 seconds, or until the watercress has wilted.

Drain the cooked pasta and return to the saucepan. Mix the salmon and watercress with the pasta. Toss the mixture using 2 large forks. Divide between 4 large serving plates and garnish with extra watercress leaves. Serve immediately.

salt and pepper

225 g/8 oz dried fettuccine

1 tsp olive oil

1 garlic clove, finely chopped

55 g/2 oz smoked salmon,
cut into thin strips

55 g/2 oz watercress leaves,
plus extra to garnish

sardine & fennel sauce

This is a very quick sauce and is ideal paired with pasta for midweek suppers because it is so simple to prepare, yet packed full of flavour. *SERVES 4*

350 g/12 oz dried linguine

2 tbsp olive oil

sprigs of fresh parsley, to garnish

sauce

8 sardines, filleted

1 fennel bulb

2 tbsp olive oil

3 garlic cloves, sliced

1 tsp chilli flakes

$^{1}/_{2}$ tsp finely grated lemon zest

1 tbsp lemon juice

2 tbsp pine kernels, toasted

2 tbsp chopped fresh parsley

salt and pepper

To make the sauce, wash the sardines and pat dry on kitchen paper. Coarsely chop them into large pieces and set aside. Trim the fennel bulb and slice very thinly.

Heat the olive oil in a large, heavy-based frying pan and add the sliced garlic and the chilli flakes. Cook for 1 minute, then add the fennel slices. Cook over a medium-high heat, stirring occasionally, for 4–5 minutes, or until softened. Lower the heat, add the sardine pieces and cook for a further 3–4 minutes, or until just cooked.

To cook the pasta, bring a saucepan of lightly salted water to the boil. Add the pasta, bring back to the boil and cook for 8–10 minutes, or until tender but still firm to the bite. Drain well and return to the pan.

Add the lemon zest and juice, pine kernels and parsley to the sauce and toss together. Season. Add the sauce to the pasta with the remaining olive oil and toss together gently. Transfer to a warmed serving dish, garnish with parsley and serve.

cook's tip

Reserve a couple of tablespoons of the pasta
cooking water and add to the pasta with the
sauce if the mixture seems a little dry.

variation

Substitute 25 g/1 oz chopped fresh basil for half the parsley, and garnish with capers instead of black olives.

tuna & anchovy sauce

The delicious parsley sauce in this recipe enhances the classic
Italian combination of pasta and tuna. *SERVES 4*

To make the sauce, remove any bones from the
tuna. Put the tuna into a food processor or blender.
Add the anchovies, oil and parsley. Process until
very smooth.

Spoon the crème fraîche into the food processor
or blender and process again for a few seconds to
blend thoroughly. Season with salt and pepper
to taste.

To cook the pasta, bring a large saucepan of
lightly salted water to the boil. Add the spaghetti
and olive oil and cook for 8–10 minutes, or until
tender but still firm to the bite.

Drain the spaghetti, return to the pan and
place over a medium heat. Add the butter and toss
well to coat. Spoon in the sauce and quickly toss
into the spaghetti, mixing well using 2 forks.

Remove the pan from the heat and divide the
spaghetti between warm individual serving plates.
Garnish with olives and parsley and serve with
warm, crusty bread.

450 g/1 lb dried spaghetti

1 tbsp olive oil

2 tbsp butter

stoned black olives, to garnish

warm crusty bread, to serve

sauce

200 g/7 oz canned tuna, drained

60 g/2¼ oz canned anchovies, drained

225 ml/8 fl oz olive oil

60 g/2¼ oz flat-leaved parsley, roughly
    chopped, plus extra to garnish

150 ml/5 fl oz crème fraîche

salt and pepper

spinach & anchovy sauce

This colourful light sauce can be paired with different types of pasta,
including fettucine, spaghetti and linguine. *SERVES 4*

400 g/14 oz dried fettucine

salt

1 tbsp olive oil

sauce

900 g/2 lb fresh, young spinach leaves

4 tbsp olive oil

3 tbsp pine kernels

3 garlic cloves, crushed

**8 canned anchovy fillets, drained
        and chopped**

To make the sauce, trim off any tough spinach stalks. Rinse the spinach leaves and then place them in a large saucepan with only the water that is clinging to them after washing. Cover and cook over a high heat, shaking the pan from time to time, until the spinach has wilted but retains its colour. Drain well, set aside and keep warm.

To cook the pasta, bring a large saucepan of lightly salted water to the boil. Add the fettucine, bring back to the boil and cook for 8–10 minutes, or until tender but still firm to the bite.

Meanwhile, going back to the sauce, heat the olive oil in a saucepan. Add the pine kernels and cook until golden. Remove the pine kernels from the pan with a slotted spoon and set aside.

Add the garlic to the pan and cook until golden. Add the anchovies and stir in the spinach. Cook, stirring constantly, for 2–3 minutes, or until heated through. Return the pine kernels to the pan.

Drain the fettucine, toss in olive oil and transfer to a warm serving dish. Spoon the anchovy and spinach sauce over the fettucine, then toss lightly and serve immediately.

cook's tip

If you are in a hurry, you can use frozen

spinach. Thaw and drain it thoroughly,

pressing out as much moisture as possible.

Cut the leaves into strips and add to the

dish with the anchovies.

pesto & anchovy sauce

This is an ideal dish for cooks in a hurry because it can be prepared in minutes from storecupboard ingredients. *SERVES 4*

6 tbsp olive oil

2 garlic cloves, crushed

60 g/2¹/₄ oz canned anchovy fillets, drained

450 g/1 lb dried spaghetti

60 g/2¹/₄ oz ready-made pesto sauce

2 tbsp finely chopped fresh oregano

salt and pepper

90 g/3¹/₄ oz grated Parmesan cheese, plus extra to garnish (optional)

sprigs of fresh oregano, to garnish

Heat 5 tablespoons of the oil in a small saucepan. Add the garlic and cook for 3 minutes.

Lower the heat, stir in the anchovies and cook, stirring occasionally, for 10–12 minutes, or until the anchovies have disintegrated.

Bring a large saucepan of lightly salted water to the boil. Add the spaghetti and the remaining olive oil and cook for 8–10 minutes, or until just tender but still firm to the bite.

Add the pesto sauce and chopped oregano to the garlic and anchovy mixture, and season with pepper to taste.

Drain the spaghetti and use a slotted spoon to transfer to a warm serving dish. Pour the pesto sauce over the spaghetti and then sprinkle over the grated Parmesan cheese.

Garnish with sprigs of fresh oregano, and extra Parmesan cheese, if using.

cook's tip
If you find canned anchovies too salty, soak them in a saucer of cold milk for 5 minutes, then drain and pat dry with kitchen paper before using. The milk absorbs the salt.

cook's tip

If you are making fresh pasta, remember
that pasta dough prefers warm conditions
and responds well to handling. Do not
leave to chill and do not use a marble
work surface for kneading.

sicilian sauce

This Sicilian sauce of anchovies mixed with pine kernels, sultanas
and tomatoes is delicious with all types of pasta. *SERVES 4*

To make the sauce, cook the tomatoes under a preheated grill for 10 minutes. Leave to cool. When cool enough to handle, peel off the skin and dice the flesh.

Place the pine kernels on a baking sheet and lightly toast under the grill for 2–3 minutes, or until golden.

Soak the sultanas in a bowl of warm water for about 20 minutes. Drain them thoroughly.

Place the tomatoes, toasted pine kernels and sultanas in a small saucepan and heat gently.

Add the anchovies and tomato purée, heating the sauce for an additional 2–3 minutes, or until hot.

To cook the pasta, place in a saucepan of lightly salted boiling water and cook according to the instructions on the packet, or until tender but still firm to the bite. Drain thoroughly.

Transfer the pasta to a serving plate and serve with the hot sauce.

675 g/1 lb 8 oz fresh penne or 350 g/12 oz dried penne

sauce
450 g/1 lb tomatoes, halved
25 g/1 oz pine kernels
50 g/1³/4 oz sultanas
50 g/1³/4 oz canned anchovies, drained and halved lengthways
2 tbsp concentrated tomato purée

creamy &
cheesy sauces

TAGLIATELLE, fettuccine, tagliarini and penne are excellent pastas for creamy and cheesy sauces. The delicious recipes included here are simple and quick to prepare and offer a diversity of flavours in their use of Parmesan, ricotta, Gorgonzola and mascarpone cheeses.

creamy cheese sauce

This simple, traditional dish can be made with any long pasta, but is especially good with flat noodles, such as fettuccine or tagliatelle. *SERVES 4*

25 g/1 oz butter
200 ml/7 fl oz double cream
450 g/1 lb fresh fettuccine
1 tbsp olive oil
85 g/3 oz Parmesan cheese, freshly grated, plus extra to serve
pinch of freshly grated nutmeg
salt and pepper
fresh parsley sprigs, to garnish

Put the butter and 150 ml/5 fl oz of the cream in a large saucepan and bring the mixture to the boil over a medium heat. Reduce the heat and then simmer gently for about 1^{1}/$_{2}$ minutes, or until slightly thickened.

Meanwhile, bring a large pan of lightly salted water to the boil. Add the fettuccine and olive oil and cook for 2–3 minutes, or until tender but still firm to the bite. Drain the fettuccine, then pour over the cream sauce.

Toss the fettuccine in the sauce over a low heat until thoroughly coated.

Add the remaining cream, the Parmesan cheese and nutmeg to the fettuccine mixture and season to taste with salt and pepper. Toss thoroughly to coat while gently heating through.

Transfer the fettucine mixture to a warm serving plate and garnish with the fresh sprigs of parsley. Serve immediately, handing round extra grated Parmesan cheese separately.

variation

This classic Roman dish is delicious
served with the addition of fresh peas.
Add 225 g/8 oz shelled cooked peas with
the Parmesan cheese.

variation

You don't have to use tagliatelle for this recipe.

You can make any type of pasta you wish.

tagliatelle
with garlic butter

Pasta is not difficult to make yourself, just a little time-consuming.
However, the resulting pasta takes only a couple of minutes to cook and
tastes wonderful. *SERVES 4*

**450 g/1 lb strong white flour,
plus extra for dusting**

2 tsp salt

4 eggs, beaten

2 tbsp olive oil

75 g/2³/4 oz butter, melted

3 garlic cloves, finely chopped

2 tbsp chopped fresh parsley

pepper

Sift the flour into a large bowl and stir in the salt. Make a well in the centre of the dry ingredients and add the eggs and the olive oil. Using a wooden spoon, stir in the eggs, gradually drawing in the flour. After a few minutes, the dough will be too stiff to use a spoon so use your fingers.

When the flour has been incorporated, turn the dough out onto a floured work surface and knead for 5 minutes. If the dough is too wet, add a little flour and continue kneading. Cover with clingfilm and leave to rest for at least 15 minutes.

Roll out the pasta thinly and create the pasta shapes required. This can be done by hand or using a pasta machine. To make the tagliatelle by hand, fold the thinly rolled pasta sheets into 3 and cut out long, thin strips, 1 cm/¹/2 inch wide.

To cook, bring a large, heavy-based saucepan of water to the boil. Add the pasta, return to the boil and cook for 2–3 minutes, or until tender but still firm to the bite. Drain.

Mix the butter, garlic and parsley together. Stir into the pasta, season with a little pepper to taste and serve immediately.

garlic, mushroom & cheese sauce

This dish can be prepared in minutes – the intense flavours are sure
to make this a popular recipe. *SERVES 4*

2 tbsp walnut oil

1 bunch spring onions, sliced

2 garlic cloves, thinly sliced

225 g/8 oz mushrooms, sliced

450 g/1 lb fresh green and white tagliatelle

225 g/8 oz frozen chopped leaf spinach,
thawed and drained

115 g/4 oz full-fat cream cheese with
garlic and herbs

4 tbsp single cream

salt and pepper

60 g/2¹/4 oz unsalted pistachio nuts, chopped

2 tbsp shredded fresh basil

sprigs of fresh basil, to garnish

fresh Italian bread, to serve

Gently heat the walnut oil in a wok or frying pan and sauté the spring onions and garlic for 1 minute, or until just soft. Add the mushrooms to the pan, stir well, cover and cook gently for 5 minutes, or until soft.

Meanwhile, bring a large saucepan of lightly salted water to the boil and cook the pasta for 3–5 minutes, or until just tender. Drain the pasta thoroughly and return to the pan.

Add the spinach to the mushrooms and heat through for 1–2 minutes. Add the cheese and let it melt slightly. Stir in the cream and continue to heat without letting it boil.

Pour the vegetable mixture over the pasta, season to taste and mix well. Heat gently, stirring, for 2–3 minutes.

Transfer the pasta into a warmed serving bowl and sprinkle over the pistachio nuts and shredded basil. Garnish with sprigs of fresh basil and serve with fresh Italian bread.

creamy mushroom sauce

This easy vegetarian sauce is ideal for busy people with little time
to spare and tastes very good! *SERVES 4*

To make the sauce, heat the butter and olive oil in a large saucepan. Add the sliced shallots and cook over a medium heat for 3 minutes. Add the mushrooms and cook over a low heat for 2 minutes. Season to taste with salt and pepper, then sprinkle over the flour and cook, stirring constantly, for 1 minute.

Gradually stir in the cream and port, then add the sun-dried tomatoes and a pinch of grated nutmeg. Cook over a low heat for 8 minutes.

Meanwhile, to cook the pasta, bring a large saucepan of lightly salted water to the boil. Add the spaghetti and olive oil and cook for 12–14 minutes, or until tender but still firm to the bite.

Drain the spaghetti and return to the pan. Pour over the mushroom sauce and cook for 3 minutes. Transfer the spaghetti and mushroom sauce to a large serving plate and sprinkle over the chopped parsley. Serve with crispy triangles of fried bread.

450 g/1 lb dried spaghetti

1 tbsp olive oil

1 tbsp coarsely chopped fresh parsley

6 triangles of fried white bread, to serve

sauce

4 tbsp butter

1 tbsp olive oil

6 shallots, sliced

450 g/1 lb button mushrooms, sliced

salt and pepper

1 tsp plain flour

150 ml/5 fl oz double cream

2 tbsp port

115 g/4 oz sun-dried tomatoes, chopped

pinch of freshly grated nutmeg

variation

If you like the sound of this recipe but do
not have any port available, you can use
2 tablespoons of dry white wine instead.

cook's tip

Use 2 large forks to toss spaghetti or other long pasta, so that it is thoroughly coated with the sauce. Special spaghetti forks are available from some cookware departments and kitchen shops.

ricotta sauce

This light pasta dish has a delicate flavour ideally suited to a summer lunch. *SERVES 4*

350 g/12 oz dried spaghetti

3 tbsp butter

2 tbsp chopped fresh flat-leaved parsley

115 g/4 oz freshly ground almonds

115 g/4 oz ricotta cheese

pinch of freshly grated nutmeg

pinch of ground cinnamon

150 ml/5 fl oz crème fraîche

2 tbsp olive oil

125 ml/4 fl oz hot chicken stock

salt and pepper

1 tbsp pine kernels

sprigs of fresh flat-leaved parsley, to garnish

Bring a saucepan of lightly salted water to the boil. Add the spaghetti, bring back to the boil and then cook for 8–10 minutes, or until tender but still firm to the bite.

Drain the pasta, return to the pan and toss with the butter and chopped parsley. Set aside and keep warm.

Combine the ground almonds, ricotta cheese, nutmeg, cinnamon and crème fraîche in a small saucepan and stir over a low heat to a thick paste. Gradually stir in the oil. When the oil has been fully incorporated, gradually stir in the hot stock until smooth. Season to taste with pepper.

Transfer the spaghetti to a warm serving dish, pour the sauce over it and toss together well (see cook's tip). Sprinkle over the pine kernels, garnish with the sprigs of fresh flat-leaved parsley and serve immediately.

tagliarini
with gorgonzola sauce

This simple, creamy pasta sauce is a classic Italian recipe. You could use
Danish blue cheese instead of the Gorgonzola, if you prefer. *SERVES 4*

25 g/1 oz butter

225 g/8 oz Gorgonzola cheese,
roughly crumbled

150 ml/5 fl oz double cream

2 tbsp dry white wine

1 tsp cornflour

4 fresh sage sprigs, finely chopped

salt and white pepper

400 g/14 oz dried tagliarini

2 tbsp olive oil

Melt the butter in a heavy-based saucepan. Stir in 175 g/6 oz of the cheese and melt, over a low heat, for about 2 minutes.

Add the cream, white wine and cornflour and beat with a whisk until fully incorporated.

Stir in the sage and season to taste with salt and white pepper. Bring to the boil over a low heat, whisking constantly, until the sauce thickens. Remove from the heat and set aside while you cook the pasta.

Bring a large saucepan of lightly salted water to the boil. Add the tagliarini and 1 tablespoon of the olive oil. Cook the pasta for 8–10 minutes, or

until just tender, then drain thoroughly and toss in the remaining olive oil. Transfer the pasta to a serving dish and keep warm.

Reheat the Gorgonzola sauce over a low heat, whisking constantly. Spoon the sauce over the tagliarini, generously sprinkle over the remaining cheese and serve.

cook's tip

When buying Gorgonzola, always check
that it is creamy yellow with delicate green
veining. Avoid hard or discoloured cheese.
It should have a rich, piquant aroma,
not a bitter smell.

blue cheese & vegetable sauce

Some of the simplest and most satisfying dishes are made with pasta, such as this
delicious combination of tagliatelle with two-cheese sauce. *SERVES 4*

**300 g/10¹/₂ oz dried tagliatelle tricolore
(plain, spinach- and tomato-flavoured
noodles)
225 g/8 oz broccoli, broken into small florets
350 g/12 oz mascarpone cheese
125 g/4¹/₂ oz blue cheese, chopped
1 tbsp chopped fresh oregano
salt and pepper
25 g/1 oz butter
sprigs of fresh oregano, to garnish
freshly grated Parmesan, to serve**

Cook the tagliatelle in plenty of boiling salted
water for 8–10 minutes, or until just tender.

Meanwhile, cook the broccoli florets in a
small amount of lightly salted, boiling water. Avoid
overcooking the broccoli, so that it retains much of
its colour and texture.

Heat the mascarpone and blue cheeses
together gently in a large saucepan until they are
melted. Stir in the oregano and season with salt
and pepper to taste.

Drain the pasta thoroughly. Return it to the
saucepan and add the butter, tossing the tagliatelle
to coat it. Drain the broccoli well and add to the
pasta with the sauce, tossing gently to mix.

Divide the pasta between 4 warmed serving
plates. Garnish with sprigs of fresh oregano and
serve with freshly grated Parmesan.

creamy butternut squash sauce

The creamy, nutty flavour of squash complements the al dente texture of the pasta perfectly. *SERVES 4*

Mix the olive oil, garlic and breadcrumbs together and spread out on a large plate. Cook in the microwave on High power for 4–5 minutes, stirring until crisp and starting to brown. Reserve.

Dice the squash, then place in a large bowl with half the water. Cover and cook on High power for 8–9 minutes, stirring occasionally. Leave to stand for 2 minutes.

Place the pasta in a large bowl, add a little salt and pour over enough boiling water to cover by 2.5 cm/1 inch. Cover and cook on High power for 5 minutes, stirring once, until the pasta is just tender but still firm to the bite. Leave to stand, covered, for 1 minute before draining.

Place the butter and onion in a large bowl. Cover and cook on High power for 3 minutes.

Using a fork, coarsely mash the squash. Add to the onion with the pasta, ham, cream, cheese, parsley and remaining water. Season generously and mix well. Cover and cook on High power for 4 minutes, or until heated through.

Transfer the pasta to a large, warmed serving dish, sprinkle with the garlic crumbs and serve.

2 tbsp olive oil

1 garlic clove, crushed

55 g/2 oz fresh white breadcrumbs

500 g/1 lb 2 oz butternut squash, peeled and deseeded

8 tbsp water

500 g/1 lb 2 oz fresh penne, or other pasta shapes

15 g/¹/₂ oz butter

1 onion, sliced

125 g/4¹/₂ oz ham, cut into strips

200 ml/7 fl oz single cream

55 g/2 oz freshly grated Cheddar cheese

2 tbsp chopped fresh parsley

salt and pepper

buttered pea
& cheese sauce

This delicious sauce is served with paglia e fieno ('straw and hay' pasta),
which refers to the colours of the pasta when mixed together. *SERVES 4*

**450 g/1 lb mixed fresh green and white
spaghetti or tagliatelle
shavings of Parmesan cheese, to garnish**

sauce
**4 tbsp butter
450 g/1 lb fresh peas, shelled
200 ml/7 fl oz double cream
55 g/2 oz Parmesan cheese, freshly grated
pinch of freshly grated nutmeg
salt and pepper**

To make the sauce, melt the butter in a large saucepan. Add the peas and cook over a low heat for 2–3 minutes.

Pour 150 ml/5 fl oz of the cream into the pan, bring to the boil and then simmer for 1–1¹/2 minutes, or until slightly thickened. Remove the pan from the heat.

Meanwhile, to cook the pasta, bring a large saucepan of lightly salted water to the boil. Add the pasta, bring back to the boil and cook for 2–3 minutes, or until just tender but still firm to the bite. Remove the pan from the heat, drain the pasta thoroughly and return to the pan.

Add the sauce to the pasta. Return the pan to the heat and add the remaining cream and the Parmesan cheese. Season to taste with nutmeg and salt and pepper.

While heating through, use 2 forks to toss the pasta gently so that it is coated with the sauce.

Transfer the pasta to a warmed serving dish and serve immediately, garnished with the shavings of Parmesan cheese.

variation

Cook 140 g/5 oz sliced button or oyster mushrooms in about 4 tablespoons of butter over a low heat for 4–5 minutes. Stir into the sauce just before adding to the pasta.

vegetable sauces

THE ten colourful vegetable sauces included here are very easy and quick to prepare. The sauces, which can be wonderfully rich, very light, sweet and even hot and spicy, will appeal to vegetarians and meat-eaters alike.

olive oil & herb sauce

This easy and satisfying Roman dish originated as a cheap meal for the impoverished, but is now a favourite in restaurants and trattorias. *SERVES 4*

125 ml/4 fl oz olive oil
3 garlic cloves, crushed
salt and pepper
450 g/1 lb fresh spaghetti
3 tbsp roughly chopped fresh parsley

Reserve 1 tablespoon of the olive oil and heat the remainder in a medium saucepan. Add the garlic and a pinch of salt and cook over a low heat, stirring constantly, until golden brown, then remove the pan from the heat. Do not allow the garlic to burn as this will taint its flavour. (If it does burn, you will have to start all over again!)

Meanwhile, bring a large saucepan of lightly salted water to the boil. Add the spaghetti and remaining olive oil and cook for 2–3 minutes, or until tender but still firm to the bite. Drain the spaghetti thoroughly and return to the pan.

Add the oil and garlic mixture to the spaghetti and toss to coat thoroughly. Season to taste with pepper, add the chopped fresh parsley and toss well to coat again.

Transfer the spaghetti to a warm serving dish and serve immediately.

cook's tip

It is worth buying the best-quality olive oil
for dishes such as this one, which make a
feature of its flavour. Extra-virgin oil is
produced from the first pressing, and has
the lowest acidity and the finest flavour.

garlic walnut sauce

This rich pasta sauce is for garlic lovers everywhere. It is quick
and easy to prepare and full of flavour. *SERVES 4*

450 g/1 lb fresh green and white tagliatelle

salt and pepper

sprigs of fresh basil, to garnish

Italian bread, such as focaccia or

ciabatta, to serve

sauce

2 tbsp walnut oil

1 bunch of spring onions, sliced

2 garlic cloves, thinly sliced

225 g/8 oz mushrooms, sliced

225 g/8 oz frozen spinach, thawed

and drained

115 g/4 oz full-fat cream cheese with garlic

and herbs

4 tbsp single cream

55 g/2 oz unsalted pistachio nuts, chopped

2 tbsp shredded fresh basil

To make the sauce, heat the walnut oil in a large frying pan. Add the spring onions and garlic and fry for 1 minute, or until just softened.

Add the mushrooms, stir well, cover and cook over a low heat for 5 minutes, or until just softened but not browned.

Meanwhile, to cook the pasta, bring a large saucepan of lightly salted water to the boil. Add the tagliatelle, bring back to the boil and cook for 3–5 minutes, or until tender but still firm to the bite. Drain thoroughly and return to the pan.

Going back to the sauce, add the spinach to the frying pan and cook for 1–2 minutes. Add the cheese and heat until slightly melted. Stir in the cream and cook gently, without letting the mixture come to the boil, until warmed through.

Pour the sauce over the pasta, season to taste with salt and pepper and mix well. Heat through gently, stirring constantly, for 2–3 minutes.

Transfer the pasta to a warmed serving dish and sprinkle with the pistachio nuts and shredded basil. Garnish with the fresh basil sprigs and serve immediately with the Italian bread of your choice.

walnut & olive sauce

This vegetarian sauce is mouthwateringly light and excellent with pasta.
The quantities given here will make a lunch for four or a starter for six. *SERVES 4–6*

450 g/1 lb fresh fettucine
2 tbsp extra-virgin olive oil
2–3 tbsp chopped fresh parsley

sauce
2 thick slices wholemeal bread,
crusts removed
300 ml/10 fl oz milk
275 g/9¹/₂ oz shelled walnuts
2 garlic cloves, minced
115 g/4 oz black olives, stoned
55 g/2 oz Parmesan cheese, freshly grated
6 tbsp extra-virgin olive oil
salt and pepper
150 ml/5 fl oz double cream

To make the sauce, put the bread in a shallow dish. Pour over the milk and soak until the liquid has been absorbed.

Spread out the walnuts on a baking sheet and toast in a preheated oven, 190°C/375°F/Gas Mark 5, for 5 minutes, or until golden. Leave to cool.

Put the soaked bread, shelled walnuts, minced garlic, black olives, grated Parmesan and olive oil in a food processor and work to make a paste. Season to taste with salt and black pepper and then stir in the double cream.

To cook the pasta, bring a large saucepan of lightly salted water to the boil. Add the fettucine and half the oil and cook for 2–3 minutes, or until tender but still firm to the bite. Drain thoroughly and toss with the remaining olive oil.

Divide the cooked fettucine between individual serving plates and spoon the walnut and olive sauce on top. Sprinkle over the fresh parsley and serve.

cook's tip

Parmesan quickly loses its pungency and bite when grated. It is better to buy small quantities and grate it yourself. Wrapped in foil, a piece will keep in the refrigerator for several months.

basil & tomato sauce

Roasting the tomatoes gives a sweeter, smoother flavour to the sauce.
Italian plum or flavia tomatoes are ideal for this dish. *SERVES 4*

2 fresh rosemary sprigs

2 garlic cloves, unpeeled

450 g/1 lb tomatoes, halved and deseeded

1 tbsp olive oil

1 tbsp sun-dried tomato paste

12 fresh basil leaves, torn into pieces,

plus extra to garnish

salt and pepper

675 g/1lb 8 oz fresh farfalle or

350 g/12 oz dried

Place the rosemary, garlic and tomatoes, skin-side up, in a shallow roasting tin and drizzle with the oil. Cook under a preheated grill for about 20 minutes, or until the tomato skins have become slightly charred.

Peel the skin from the tomatoes. Roughly chop the tomato flesh and place in a saucepan. Squeeze the pulp from the garlic cloves and mix with the tomato flesh and sun-dried tomato paste. Discard the rosemary. Stir the basil into the sauce. Season with salt and pepper to taste.

Cook the farfalle in a saucepan of boiling water, according to the packet instructions or until it is cooked through but still has bite. Drain the farfalle thoroughly.

Gently heat the tomato and basil sauce until warmed through.

Transfer the farfalle to serving plates and serve with the sauce, garnished with fresh basil leaves.

cook's tip

This sauce tastes just as good served
cold in a pasta salad.

variation

Try using a different shape of pasta, such as penne, for this recipe, then put it in an ovenproof dish, top with some grated cheese and bake for a warming winter feast.

spicy tomato sauce

This deliciously fresh and slightly spicy tomato sauce is excellent
with pasta and makes a satisfying lunch or light supper. *SERVES 4*

To make the sauce, melt the butter in a saucepan.
Add the onion and garlic and cook over a low heat
for 3–4 minutes.

Add the chillies and continue cooking for
a further 2 minutes.

Add the tomatoes and stock, then lower
the heat and simmer, stirring occasionally, for
10 minutes.

Pour the sauce into a food processor and then
blend for 1 minute, or until smooth. Alternatively,
push the sauce through a sieve.

Return the sauce to the pan and add the
tomato purée, sugar and salt and pepper to taste.
Gently reheat over a low heat until piping hot.

To cook the pasta, put the tagliatelle in a
saucepan of boiling water and cook according to
the instructions on the packet, or until tender but
still firm to the bite. Drain and transfer to serving
plates. Serve immediately with the tomato sauce.

675 g/1 lb 8 oz fresh green and white
    tagliatelle, or 350 g/12 oz dried pasta

sauce

3 tbsp butter

1 onion, finely chopped

1 garlic clove, crushed

2 small red chillies, deseeded and diced

450 g/1 lb fresh tomatoes, skinned,
    deseeded and diced

200 ml/7 fl oz vegetable stock

2 tbsp tomato purée

1 tsp sugar

salt and pepper

mediterranean sauce

Delicious Mediterranean vegetables, cooked in rich tomato
sauce, make an ideal topping for nutty wholewheat pasta. *SERVES 4*

350 g/12 oz dried wholewheat spaghetti

1 tbsp olive oil

2 tbsp butter

sprigs of fresh basil, to garnish

olive bread, to serve

sauce

1 tbsp olive oil

1 large red onion, chopped

2 garlic cloves, finely chopped

1 tbsp lemon juice

4 baby aubergines, cut into quarters

600 ml/1 pint passata

salt and pepper

2 tsp caster sugar

2 tbsp tomato purée

**400 g/14 oz canned artichoke hearts,
drained and halved**

115 g/4 oz black olives, stoned

To make the sauce, heat the oil in a large frying pan. Add the onion, garlic, lemon juice and aubergines and cook over a low heat for 4–5 minutes, or until the onion and aubergines become lightly golden.

Pour in the passata, season to taste with salt and black pepper, and stir in the caster sugar and tomato purée. Bring to the boil, then lower the heat and simmer, stirring occasionally, for 20 minutes.

Gently stir in the artichoke hearts and black olives and cook for 5 minutes.

Meanwhile, cook the pasta. Bring a large saucepan of lightly salted water to the boil. Add the spaghetti and oil and cook for 7–8 minutes, or until tender but still firm to the bite.

Drain the spaghetti and toss with the butter. Transfer the spaghetti to a large serving dish.

Pour the vegetable sauce over the spaghetti and garnish with the sprigs of fresh basil. Serve immediately with olive bread.

fragrant aubergine sauce

Prepare the marinated aubergines well in advance so that, when you are ready to eat, all you have to do is cook the pasta. *SERVES 4*

150 ml/5 fl oz vegetable stock

150 ml/5 fl oz white wine vinegar

2 tsp balsamic vinegar

3 tbsp olive oil

sprig of fresh oregano

450 g/1 lb aubergines, peeled and thinly sliced

400 g/14 oz dried linguine

marinade

2 tbsp extra-virgin olive oil

2 garlic cloves, crushed

2 tbsp chopped fresh oregano

2 tbsp finely chopped roasted almonds

2 tbsp diced red pepper

2 tbsp lime juice

grated rind and juice of 1 orange

salt and pepper

Put the vegetable stock, wine vinegar and balsamic vinegar into a saucepan and bring to the boil over a low heat. Add 2 teaspoons of the olive oil and the sprig of fresh oregano and simmer gently for about 1 minute.

Add the aubergine slices to the pan, remove from the heat and set aside for 10 minutes.

Meanwhile, to make the marinade, combine the oil, garlic, fresh oregano, almonds, red pepper, lime juice, and orange rind and juice in a large bowl and season to taste with salt and pepper.

Using a slotted spoon, carefully remove the aubergine slices from the pan and drain well. Add the aubergine to the marinade, mixing well to coat. Cover with clingfilm and set aside in the refrigerator for about 12 hours.

To cook the pasta, bring a large saucepan of lightly salted water to the boil. Add half of the remaining oil and the linguine. Bring back to the boil and cook for 8–10 minutes, or until just tender but still firm to the bite.

Drain the pasta thoroughly and toss with the remaining oil while it is still warm. Arrange the pasta on a serving plate with the aubergine slices and the marinade and serve immediately.

variation

Add 2 tablespoons of red wine vinegar to the sauce and use as a dressing for a cold pasta salad, if you wish.

chilli & red pepper sauce

This roasted red pepper and chilli sauce is sweet and spicy – the perfect combination for those who like to add just a little spice to life! *SERVES 4*

675 g/1 lb 8 oz fresh pasta
or 350 g/12 oz dried pasta
fresh oregano leaves, to garnish

sauce
2 red peppers, halved and deseeded
1 small, fresh, red chilli
4 tomatoes, halved
2 garlic cloves
55 g/2 oz ground almonds
100 ml/3¹/₂ fl oz olive oil

To make the sauce, place the red peppers, skin side up, on a baking sheet with the chilli and tomatoes. Cook under a preheated grill for 15 minutes, or until charred. After 10 minutes, turn the tomatoes over, skin side up. Put the peppers and chillies in a plastic bag and set aside for 10 minutes.

Peel the skins from the red peppers and chilli and slice the flesh into strips. Peel the garlic, and peel and deseed the tomato halves.

Place the ground almonds on a baking sheet and place under the grill for 2–3 minutes until golden.

In a food processor, process the red peppers, chilli, garlic and tomatoes to make a purée. With the motor still running, slowly add the olive oil through the feeder tube to form a thick sauce. Alternatively, mash the mixture with a fork and beat in the olive oil, drop by drop.

Stir the toasted ground almonds into the mixture. Warm the sauce in a pan until it is heated.

To cook the pasta, bring a large saucepan of lightly salted water to the boil. Add the pasta, bring back to the boil and cook for 3–5 minutes if using fresh pasta or 8–10 minutes if using dried pasta. Drain well and transfer to a serving dish. Pour over the sauce and toss to mix. Garnish with the fresh oregano leaves and serve.

green vegetable sauce

The different shapes and textures of the vegetables make a mouthwatering presentation in this light and summery dish. *SERVES 4*

225 g/8 oz dried gemelli or other dried pasta shapes

1 head broccoli, cut into florets

2 courgettes, sliced

225 g/8 oz asparagus spears

115 g/4 oz mangetout

115 g/4 oz frozen peas

25 g/1 oz butter

3 tbsp vegetable stock

4 tbsp double cream

salt and pepper

freshly grated nutmeg

2 tbsp chopped fresh parsley

2 tbsp fresh Parmesan cheese shavings

Bring a large saucepan of lightly salted water to the boil over a medium heat. Add the pasta and cook for 8–10 minutes, or until tender but still firm to the bite. Drain thoroughly, return to the saucepan, cover and keep warm.

Steam the broccoli, courgettes, asparagus spears and mangetout over a saucepan of boiling salted water until they are just starting to soften. Remove from the heat and refresh in cold water. Drain and reserve.

Bring a small saucepan of lightly salted water to the boil over a medium heat. Add the frozen peas and cook for 3 minutes. Drain the peas, refresh in cold water, then drain again. Reserve with the other vegetables.

Heat the butter and vegetable stock in a saucepan over a medium heat. Add all of the vegetables, reserving a few of the asparagus spears, and toss carefully with a wooden spoon until they have heated through, taking care not to break them up.

Stir in the cream and heat through without bringing to the boil. Season to taste with salt, pepper and nutmeg.

Transfer the pasta to a warmed serving dish and stir in the chopped parsley. Spoon over the vegetable sauce and sprinkle over the Parmesan cheese. Arrange the reserved asparagus spears in a pattern on the top and serve.

cook's tip

You can use lime juice instead of the
lemon juice. Since limes are usually
smaller, squeeze the juice from 2 fruits.

hot courgette sauce

This is a really fresh-tasting sauce, made with courgettes and cream.
This dish is ideal with a crisp white wine and some crusty bread. *SERVES 4*

To make the sauce, use a swivel-bladed vegetable peeler to slice the courgettes into thin ribbons.

Heat the oil in a frying pan and cook the garlic for 30 seconds.

Add the courgettes and cook over a low heat, stirring, for 5–7 minutes.

Stir in the basil, chillies, lemon juice, cream and Parmesan and season to taste. Keep warm over a very low heat.

To cook the pasta, bring a large saucepan of lightly salted water to the boil. Add the pasta, bring back to the boil and cook for 8–10 minutes, or until tender but still firm to the bite. Drain thoroughly and put the pasta in a warm serving bowl.

Pile the courgette sauce on top of the pasta and serve with crusty bread.

225 g/8 oz dried tagliatelle
crusty bread, to serve

sauce
675 g/1 lb 8 oz courgettes
6 tbsp olive oil
3 garlic cloves, crushed
3 tbsp chopped fresh basil
2 fresh red chillies, deseeded and sliced
juice of 1 large lemon
5 tbsp single cream
4 tbsp grated Parmesan cheese
salt and pepper

index

A

anchovies
    Sicilian sauce 53
    spinach sauce 48
    pesto sauce 50
    tuna sauce 47
asparagus, green vegetable sauce 92
aubergines
    fragrant sauce 89
    Mediterranean sauce 86

B

bacon
    tomato & mushroom sauce 25
basic tomato sauce 7
basil & tomato sauce 82
Bolognese sauce 10
broccoli, green vegetable sauce 92
bucatini with lamb & yellow pepper
    sauce 16
butternut squash, creamy sauce 71

C

carbonara sauce 20
carrots, prawn & vegetable sauce 31
cauliflower, prawn & vegeable sauce 31
cheese
    blue cheese & vegetable sauce 69
    creamy sauce 56
    garlic & mushroom sauce 60
    Parmesan 81
    ricotta sauce 65
    tagliarini with Gorgonzola sauce 66
chicken
    creamy sauce 19
    livers 11
chilli & red pepper sauce 91
clam sauce 37
courgettes
    hot sauce 95
    green vegetable sauce 92
    prawn & vegetable sauce 31
crab, spicy sauce 32
cream
    butternut squash sauce 71
    chicken sauce 19
    cheese sauce 56
    mushroom sauce 62
    smoked salmon sauce 41

E

egg 21

F

farfalle 82
fennel, & sardine sauce 44
fettucine 43, 48, 56, 80

G

garlic
    mushroom & cheese sauce 60
    tagliatelle with butter 59
    walnut sauce 79
gemelli 92
Gorgonzola 67
    tagliarini with sauce 66
green vegetable sauce 92

H

herbs, olive oil sauce 76

L

lamb, bucatini with yellow pepper sauce 16
linguine 44, 89

M

mangetout
    green vegetable sauce 92
    prawn & vegetable sauce 31
meatballs, tarragon sauce 13
Mediterranean sauce 86
mushrooms 73
    creamy sauce 62
    garlic & cheese sauce 60
    tomatoes & bacon sauce 25
mussels, saffron sauce 34

O

olive oil 77
    & herb sauce 76
olives, & walnut sauce 80

P

paglia e fieno 72
Parma ham, pumpkin sauce 23
pasta, fresh 52
peas 57
    & cheese sauce 72
    green vegetable sauce 92
penne 53, 71, 84
peppers
    chilli & red pepper sauce 91
    bucatini with lamb & yellow pepper
      sauce 16
pesto & anchovy sauce 50
pine kernels, Sicilian sauce 53
prawn & vegetable sauce 31
pumpkin sauce with Parma ham 23

R

red seafood sauce 29
rocket 42
ricotta sauce 65
rigatoni with squid sauce 38

S

saffron mussel sauce 34
salad, pasta 83, 90
salmon, smoked
    cream sauce 41
    & watercress sauce 43
sardine & fennel sauce 44
seafood sauce 28
Sicilian sauce 53
spaghetti 10, 13, 20, 31, 37, 41, 47, 50, 62, 65,
    72, 76, 86
spaghetti forks 64
spaghettini 32
spicy crab sauce 32
spinach 49
    & anchovy sauce 48
squid sauce, with rigatoni 38
sultanas, Sicilian sauce 53

T

tagliarini with Gorgonzola sauce 66
tagliatelle 14, 19, 23, 34, 56, 60, 69, 72, 79,
    85, 95
    with garlic butter 59
tarragon meatball sauce 13
tomatoes 39
    basil sauce 82
    mushroom & bacon sauce 25
    Sicilian sauce 53
    spicy sauce 85
    sun-dried sauce 14
tuna & anchovy sauce 47

V

vegetable
    blue cheese sauce 69
    green vegetable sauce 92
    & prawn sauce 31
vermicelli 37

W

walnut
    garlic sauce 79
    & olive sauce 80
watercress, & smoked salmon sauce 43